Becoming The Next Warren Buffett

Applying Warren's Principles, Ideas
and Strategies to your Life

Oliver Wealthford

Contents

Introduction

In the realm of finance and investing, one name shines brighter than most: Warren Buffett. His journey from a modest upbringing in Omaha, Nebraska, to becoming one of the world's wealthiest and most respected investors has captivated the imaginations of countless individuals seeking financial success and wisdom. For decades, Warren Buffett has been heralded as the "Oracle of Omaha," a moniker that underscores his extraordinary ability to navigate the complex world of stocks, bonds, and businesses with unparalleled expertise.

But what is it about Warren Buffett that sets him apart from the rest? Is it simply luck, a mysterious gift, or perhaps a secret recipe hidden away in some dusty old vault? The truth is, there is no secret sauce, no magic formula, and no shortcut to becoming the next Warren Buffett. Instead, there is something more profound at play: a set of timeless principles and a way of thinking that anyone can learn and apply.

This book, "Becoming Warren Buffett: How to Be Like Warren Buffett," is not just a biography of a financial titan. It is a roadmap for you, the reader, to embark on your own journey to financial success, armed with the knowledge and strategies that have made Warren Buffett an icon. Through the pages that follow, we will delve into the life, principles, and investment strategies of Warren Buffett, breaking down the complexities of his approach into practical steps that you can implement in your own life.

So, if you've ever wondered how to be like Warren Buffett, join us on this journey. Discover the principles that have guided his remarkable success and learn how to apply them to your own life. Together, we will explore the strategies, the wisdom, and the mindset that can help you become the next Warren Buffett.

Chapter 1: Warren Buffett's Early Life and Influences

Warren Buffett's upbringing and early experiences

Warren Edward Buffett, one of the most successful investors of all time, was not born with a silver spoon in his mouth. In fact, his early life was characterized by modest beginnings and a relentless pursuit of knowledge. To truly understand the man and his remarkable journey to financial prowess, we must delve into the origins of the Oracle of Omaha.

A Humble Beginning

Warren Buffett was born on August 30, 1930, in Omaha, Nebraska. He was the second of three children in the Buffett family. His father, Howard Buffett, was a stockbroker and U.S. Congressman, and his mother, Leila Buffett, was a homemaker. Despite his father's profession, young Warren's interest in finance didn't manifest itself immediately.

Growing up, Warren displayed an entrepreneurial spirit from a young age. He began delivering newspapers at the tender age of 13, eventually building a sizable clientele and saving his earnings diligently. It was here that he got his first taste of the business world, realizing the power of compound interest, an insight that would shape his investment philosophy in the years to come.

Mentors and Early Influence

While his father's career offered some exposure to the world of stocks, it was Ben Graham's book, "The Intelligent Investor," that had a profound impact on Warren Buffett. Graham, a renowned economist and investor, introduced the concept of value investing, which became the cornerstone of Buffett's approach to the markets. Buffett often refers to this book as the most important he ever read and cherishes his copy with hand-written notes and annotations.

Buffett's insatiable appetite for learning also led him to the Columbia Business School, where he studied under Graham himself. The mentorship of Ben Graham was transformative for Buffett, providing him with the intellectual foundation and discipline needed for a successful career in finance.

The Early Lessons

During his early years, Warren Buffett experimented with various business ventures, including pinball machines and selling golf balls. These experiences taught him invaluable lessons about risk, profit, and entrepreneurship. He discovered that careful analysis and a

keen understanding of the market were ·
essential for any venture to succeed.

As we delve further into Warren
Buffett's journey, you will see how these
early experiences and influences laid the
groundwork for his future success. But
perhaps the most important lesson to
take from his humble beginnings is that
greatness can emerge from the most
unassuming of origins. Buffett's story is
a testament to the power of
perseverance, passion for learning, and
an unwavering commitment to his
principles.

Chapter 2: Unpacking Warren Buffett's Strategies

The Oracle's Toolkit: Buffett's Investment Principles

Warren Buffett's investment philosophy can be distilled into a few core principles that serve as the foundation of his success:

1. Value Investing: At the heart of Buffett's approach is value investing. He seeks out companies that are undervalued by the market, trading at

prices below their intrinsic worth. This contrarian mindset allows him to buy low and hold for the long term.

2. Economic Moats: Buffett often refers to the concept of an economic moat, which represents a company's competitive advantage. He looks for businesses with durable competitive advantages, such as strong brand recognition, cost leadership, or network effects.

3. Margin of Safety: One of Buffett's cardinal rules is to invest with a margin of safety. This means buying stocks at a significant discount to their intrinsic value, providing a cushion against unexpected downturns.

4. Long-Term Perspective: Buffett's investments are typically held for the long haul. He believes in the power of compounding and the benefits of patience in letting investments grow over time.

5. Quality over Quantity: Contrary to the popular notion of diversification, Buffett advocates for concentrated investing in a few high-quality companies. He believes in thoroughly understanding each investment and its potential risks.

The Berkshire Hathaway Model

Warren Buffett's investment vehicle, Berkshire Hathaway, serves as a prime example of his principles in action. Under his leadership, Berkshire Hathaway has grown into one of the largest and most successful conglomerates in the world.

- Acquisitions: Buffett is known for acquiring entire companies, often well-established and with strong moats. He looks for businesses that fit into Berkshire's portfolio and can benefit from its resources.

- Stock Portfolio: Berkshire Hathaway's stock portfolio includes a carefully selected mix of stocks from various industries. These investments are chosen based on their alignment with Buffett's value and quality criteria.

- Insurance Operations: The insurance business has been a cornerstone of Berkshire Hathaway's success, providing a stable source of capital for investments. Buffett's expertise in insurance underwriting has contributed significantly to the company's growth.

Buffett's Track Record: Proof in the Pudding

Warren Buffett's investment prowess is best illustrated by his track record. Over several decades, he has consistently outperformed the broader market indices, turning Berkshire Hathaway into a compounding machine of wealth.

Key Takeaways

As we conclude this chapter, it's essential to recognize that Warren Buffett's investment strategies are not limited to the realm of finance; they embody timeless principles that can be applied to various aspects of life. His disciplined approach to value, quality, and patience serves as an inspiration for those seeking to build enduring wealth and financial security. In the following chapters, we will explore how you can adopt these principles and apply them to your own financial journey, becoming the next Warren Buffett in your own right.

Chapter 3: Long-Term Wealth: The Art of Patient Investing

Warren Buffett's enduring success as an investor can be attributed, in large part, to his unwavering commitment to the principles of patient investing. In a world where quick gains and instant gratification often take precedence, Buffett's approach stands as a testament to the power of long-term thinking.

The Importance of Long-Term Thinking

Before we go into specifics of Warren Buffett's investment strategies, it's crucial to understand why patience matters. The stock market, like life itself, is filled with ups and downs. Prices fluctuate daily, influenced by news, rumors, and market sentiment. It's easy to get caught up in the frenzy of short-term gains and losses, but Buffett's success reminds us that real wealth is built over time.

1. Compound Interest: The Eighth Wonder of the World

Buffett once called compound interest "the eighth wonder of the world." This simple yet profound concept highlights the exponential growth potential of money invested wisely. We'll explore how compounding works and why it's a cornerstone of Buffett's strategy.

2. The Psychology of Patience

Warren Buffett often emphasizes that the stock market is a place where the patient investor thrives while the impatient speculator falters. We'll delve into the psychological aspects of patience, including the ability to resist impulsive decisions driven by fear or greed.

Strategies for Building Wealth Over Time

Now that we understand the importance of patience, let's discuss how to apply this principle to your investment journey. Warren Buffett's approach to long-term wealth creation is based on several key strategies.

1. Buy and Hold

Buffett is a renowned proponent of the "buy and hold" strategy. We'll explore why he advocates holding onto quality stocks for extended periods and the benefits it brings, including reduced trading costs and taxes.

2. Focus on Quality, Not Quantity

One of Buffett's famous sayings is, "It's far better to buy a wonderful company at a fair price than a fair company at a wonderful price." We'll discuss how to identify companies with enduring competitive advantages, also known as economic moats.

3. Diversification with a Purpose

While Buffett believes in focusing on a few carefully chosen investments, he also recognizes the importance of diversification. We'll examine how to strike the right balance and avoid over-diversification, a common mistake that can dilute returns.

Staying Committed to Long-Term Goals

Patience isn't just about waiting; it's about staying committed to your long-term goals, even when faced with adversity. In this section, we'll provide tips on how to maintain your resolve and navigate the inevitable challenges of the investing journey.

1. Setting Realistic Expectations

Buffett advises investors to expect fluctuations and temporary setbacks. We'll discuss how having realistic expectations can help you stay the course during market turbulence.

2. The Power of Dollar-Cost Averaging

Dollar-cost averaging is a technique that involves investing a fixed amount of money at regular intervals, regardless of market conditions. We'll explain how this strategy can reduce the impact of market volatility and make investing more systematic.

3. Review and Adjust

Even long-term investors like Warren Buffett periodically review their portfolios and adjust their strategies. We'll outline when and how to make thoughtful adjustments to your investments.

In this chapter, we've explored the significance of patient investing and the strategies that Warren Buffett has employed to build long-term wealth. Remember, the road to financial success is not a sprint; it's a marathon. Embracing the art of patience can make all the difference in your journey to becoming the next Warren Buffett.

Chapter 4: Lessons Directly from Warren Buffett

Warren Buffett has accumulated a wealth of knowledge and experience throughout his legendary career. In this chapter, we will delve into some of the most profound lessons and insights directly from the man himself. These nuggets of wisdom offer a glimpse into the mind of one of the most successful investors in history and can serve as guiding principles for your own journey to financial success.

Lessons and Quotes

Warren Buffett is known for his straightforward and insightful advice. Here are some of his most memorable lessons and quotes:

Lesson 1: "Rule No. 1: Never lose money. Rule No. 2: Never forget Rule No. 1."

This simple yet powerful mantra encapsulates Buffett's emphasis on capital preservation. He believes that avoiding significant losses is the key to long-term success. While no investment is entirely risk-free, Buffett's approach to risk management revolves around minimizing the chance of permanent capital impairment.

Lesson 2: "The stock market is designed to transfer money from the Active to the Patient."

This statement underscores Buffett's belief in the virtue of patience when it comes to investing. He often advises against frequent trading and market timing, instead advocating for a buy-and-hold strategy. By staying invested for the long haul, you can harness the power of compounding and allow your investments to grow steadily over time.

Lesson 3: "It's far better to buy a wonderful company at a fair price than a fair company at a wonderful price."

Buffett's focus on the quality of investments is evident in this quote. He values strong, well-managed companies with durable competitive advantages, even if their stock prices are not deeply discounted. This approach aligns with his commitment to long-term value creation.

Lesson 4: "Diversification is a protection against ignorance. It makes little sense if you know what you are doing."

Buffett's views on diversification are often misunderstood. He acknowledges the importance of diversification for less experienced investors but believes that knowledgeable investors can concentrate their portfolios in their best ideas. His emphasis is on understanding your investments thoroughly rather than spreading yourself too thin.

Real-Life Anecdotes

To illustrate these lessons in action, let's explore a couple of real-life anecdotes from Warren Buffett's career:

The Salomon Brothers Rescue

In the late 1980s, Warren Buffett stepped in to rescue Salomon Brothers, a major Wall Street investment bank, when it faced a crisis due to a bond-trading scandal. His swift action demonstrated his commitment to protecting his investments and his belief in the importance of ethical conduct in business.

The Coca-Cola Investment

Buffett's long-term investment in The Coca-Cola Company is a classic example of his patience and conviction. He began buying Coca-Cola shares in 1988 and continued to hold them for decades, allowing the value of his investment to compound significantly over time.

This chapter provides readers with valuable insights directly from Warren Buffett, emphasizing his core principles and illustrating them with real-life examples from his career. It sets the stage for the practical application of these lessons in the following chapters.

Chapter 5: Applying Warren's Principles to Your Life

Warren Buffett's life and investment success serve as an inspiring blueprint for anyone aspiring to achieve financial greatness. In this chapter, we'll delve into the practical steps and strategies that will help you apply Warren's principles to your own life. Whether you're just starting your investment journey or looking to refine your financial approach, these insights will set you on the path to becoming the next Warren Buffett.

Building Your Investment Portfolio: A Buffett-Inspired Blueprint

Creating a successful investment portfolio begins with a solid foundation. Warren Buffett's portfolio is legendary for its simplicity and effectiveness. By following these steps, you can build your own Buffett-inspired investment portfolio:

1. Diversification: Warren advocates for a concentrated portfolio of businesses you understand well. Learn how to strike the right balance between diversification and concentration.

2. Long-Term Focus: Embrace the power of long-term thinking. Develop the patience to weather market fluctuations and hold investments for the long haul.

Value Investing Demystified: Finding Undervalued Stocks

Warren Buffett's value investing philosophy is at the core of his success. This section explores the principles behind value investing and how to apply them:

1. Intrinsic Value: Understand the concept of intrinsic value and how to determine it. Learn to identify stocks trading below their intrinsic value.

2. Margin of Safety: Discover the importance of a margin of safety in investing. Learn how to protect your investments by buying with a margin of safety.

The Power of Patience: Mastering Long-Term Investing

Buffett's legendary patience is a key to his investment success. This section teaches you how to cultivate patience in your investment approach:

1. Avoiding Impulsivity: Learn techniques to resist the urge to buy and sell impulsively in response to market fluctuations.

2. Staying Informed: Understand the difference between patience and

complacency. Discover how to stay informed about your investments without overreacting.

Risk Management à la Buffett: Protecting Your Investments

Warren Buffett is known for his aversion to unnecessary risks. Here, we explore his approach to risk management:

1. Identifying Risks: Learn how to identify and evaluate risks associated with your investments.

2. Portfolio Diversification: Explore strategies for diversifying your portfolio to spread risk effectively.

Learning from Mistakes: Warren's Investment Blunders and Lessons

Even the Oracle of Omaha makes mistakes. In this section, we analyze some of Warren Buffett's investment blunders and extract valuable lessons:

1. Admitting Mistakes: Understand the importance of acknowledging and learning from your investment mistakes.

2. Course Correction: Discover how to pivot and make informed decisions after a misstep.

This chapter provides readers with an overview of what it takes to apply Warren Buffett's principles to their own lives, setting the stage for a deeper dive into each topic in subsequent chapters.

Chapter 6: Building Your Investment Portfolio

Warren Buffett's success as an investor is not merely a result of his intuition or luck. It's rooted in a well-thought-out approach to constructing an investment portfolio. In this chapter, we'll delve into the blueprint that can help you build your investment portfolio, drawing inspiration from the Oracle of Omaha himself.

The Foundation of a Sound Portfolio

Before you start investing, it's essential to establish a solid foundation for your portfolio. This includes:

1. Clear Financial Goals

- Define your financial objectives, whether it's saving for retirement, buying a home, or funding your children's education.

- Warren Buffett's emphasis on clarity of goals and objectives.

2. Risk Tolerance Assessment

- Evaluate your risk tolerance level. How comfortable are you with market fluctuations and potential losses?

- Buffett's emphasis on not investing in something you don't understand.

3. Diversification Strategy

- Understand the concept of diversification and how it spreads risk.

- Buffett's principles of focusing on what you know and concentrating your investments in areas of expertise.

Identifying Investment Opportunities

Warren Buffett's investment strategy revolves around identifying undervalued companies with strong fundamentals. Here's how you can follow suit:

1. Fundamental Analysis

- Learn the basics of fundamental analysis, including financial statements, ratios, and earnings reports.

- How Buffett scrutinizes a company's financials and competitive advantage.

2. Economic Moats

- Understand the concept of an economic moat, which refers to a company's sustainable competitive advantage.

- Examples from Buffett's investments in companies with wide moats.

3. Buy and Hold Approach

- Embrace the long-term perspective: Why holding onto investments can lead to better returns.

- Warren Buffett's famous quote: "Our favorite holding period is forever."

Constructing Your Portfolio

Now that you've laid the groundwork and identified investment opportunities, it's time to assemble your portfolio:

1. Stock Selection

- Tips for selecting individual stocks that align with your investment goals and risk tolerance.

- The importance of aligning with companies you believe in, as Warren Buffett often does.

2. Asset Allocation

- Define how much of your portfolio will be allocated to stocks, bonds, and other asset classes.

- Buffett's allocation choices and their rationale.

3. Rebalancing Strategy

- Develop a strategy for periodically rebalancing your portfolio to maintain your desired asset allocation.

- Insights from Buffett on adapting to changing market conditions.

Monitoring and Learning

Warren Buffett's investment journey has been marked by continuous learning and adaptability. In this section, we'll discuss:

1. Portfolio Monitoring

- The importance of keeping a watchful eye on your investments.

- Warren Buffett's disciplined approach to staying informed.

2. Learning from Success and Failure

- How to extract valuable lessons from your investment experiences.

- Buffett's ability to adapt and improve his strategies over time.

The Path Forward

Building an investment portfolio inspired by Warren Buffett is a long-term endeavor. It requires patience, discipline, and ongoing education. As you embark on this journey, remember that while Buffett's principles can guide you, your unique circumstances and goals will shape your own path to financial success.

This chapter provides readers with practical guidance on how to construct an investment portfolio inspired by Buffett's principles, emphasizing the importance of setting clear goals, understanding risk, and adopting a disciplined approach to investing.

Chapter 7: Value Investing Demystified: Finding Undervalued Stocks

Warren Buffett didn't amass his fortune by chasing after the latest fads or blindly following market trends. Instead, he adhered to a time-tested philosophy: the art of value investing. In this chapter, we will delve into the principles that underpin value investing and reveal how you can identify undervalued stocks just like Warren Buffett.

Understanding the Essence of Value Investing

Value investing isn't about predicting short-term market movements or jumping on the latest hot stock. It's about assessing the intrinsic value of a company and investing when its stock price falls below that value. This approach requires patience, discipline, and a keen eye for fundamentals.

Principle 1: Fundamental Analysis

At the heart of value investing is fundamental analysis. This involves scrutinizing a company's financial health, examining its balance sheet, income statement, and cash flow statement. By understanding the company's financials, you can gauge its true worth.

Principle 2: Margin of Safety

Warren Buffett often talks about the importance of a margin of safety. This is the difference between the intrinsic value of a stock and its market price. Investing with a margin of safety protects you from unforeseen market fluctuations and decreases your risk.

Strategies for Evaluating Potential Investment

Now that we've established the core principles, let's explore practical strategies for finding undervalued stocks:

Strategy 1: Price-to-Earnings (P/E) Ratio

The P/E ratio is a commonly used metric for evaluating stocks. It measures the relationship between a company's stock price and its earnings per share (EPS). A low P/E ratio relative to the industry average may indicate an undervalued stock.

Strategy 2: Price-to-Book (P/B) Ratio

The P/B ratio compares a company's stock price to its book value per share. A P/B ratio less than 1 suggests that the stock may be undervalued.

Strategy 3: Dividend Yield

Companies that pay dividends can provide steady income for investors. A high dividend yield combined with a history of consistent dividend payments may be a sign of a strong, undervalued company.

Strategy 4: Earnings Growth Potential

Consider a company's long-term earnings growth potential. Companies with sustainable growth prospects can provide significant returns over time.

Case Studies: Real-Life Examples

To illustrate these strategies in action, we'll delve into real-life case studies of companies that Warren Buffett has invested in. We'll analyze why he saw value in these companies and how his approach to value investing played out.

Your Path to Value Investing Success

Remember that value investing long-term endeavor. Patience and discipline are your allies. It's not about frequent trading but making well-informed decisions based on solid analysis.

This chapter provides an introduction to the principles and strategies of value investing, offering readers valuable insights and practical guidance on how to identify undervalued stocks.

Chapter 8: The Power of Patience: Mastering Long-Term Investing

Warren Buffett once quipped, "The stock market is designed to transfer money from the Active to the Patient." These words encapsulate a fundamental aspect of his investment philosophy: the power of patience. In this chapter, we'll delve into why patience is a cornerstone of Warren Buffett's success and how you can harness it to master long-term investing.

Understanding the Long Game

Patience in investing isn't merely the ability to wait; it's the capacity to stay disciplined and maintain your investment strategy despite short-term market fluctuations. Warren Buffett is renowned for his buy-and-hold approach, and this strategy has paid off handsomely over the decades.

- Time as an Advantage: Buffett's long-term perspective allows him to weather market storms and capitalize on the compounding of returns over time. We'll explore how time can work in your favor.

Resisting the Urge to Tinker

One of the challenges of long-term investing is resisting the urge to constantly buy and sell based on short-term news or market volatility. Buffett's discipline in this regard has been a key driver of his success.

- The Cost of Trading: We'll discuss how frequent trading can erode returns through transaction costs and taxes.

Compound Interest: The Eighth Wonder of the World

Buffett has often spoken of compound interest as "the eighth wonder of the world." We'll break down this concept, showing how it can turbocharge your investments over time.

- The Snowball Effect: Learn how even modest investments can grow exponentially with patience and consistent contributions.

Behavioral Challenges

Patience is a virtue, but it's not always easy to maintain. We'll explore common behavioral biases that can tempt investors to deviate from their long-term plans and how to overcome them.

- Overcoming Fear and Greed: Buffett advises being "fearful when others are greedy and greedy when others are fearful." We'll discuss how this principle applies to patient investing.

Creating Your Long-Term Investment Plan

To master long-term investing, you need a well-defined plan that aligns with your financial goals and risk tolerance. We'll guide you through the steps to create your own long-term investment strategy.

- Setting Goals: How to define your financial objectives and time horizon.

- Asset Allocation: Crafting a diversified portfolio that suits your goals and risk tolerance.

- Sticking to Your Plan: Strategies for maintaining discipline and not succumbing to market noise.

Case Studies in Patience

Throughout this chapter, we'll examine real-world examples of Buffett's long-term investments, showcasing how patience and conviction paid off. These case studies will offer valuable insights into the practical application of patient investing.

In the world of investing, patience truly is a virtue that can lead to financial prosperity. By the end of this chapter, you'll have a solid understanding of why patience matters, how it has contributed to Warren Buffett's success, and practical strategies for mastering the art of long-term investing.

Chapter 9: Risk Management à la Buffett: Protecting Your Investments

In the world of investing, risk is an ever-present companion. However, Warren Buffett has shown us that prudent risk management can make all the difference between financial success and failure. In this chapter, we delve into the strategies Buffett employs to safeguard his investments and how you can apply them to your own portfolio.

The Berkshire Hathaway Annual Letter

Warren Buffett is known for his annual letters to shareholders of Berkshire Hathaway, and within these letters lies a treasure trove of insights on risk management. Buffett emphasizes the importance of understanding the businesses you invest in thoroughly. He famously quips that his ideal holding period for a stock is "forever." This perspective underscores his commitment to long-term investing as a risk management strategy.

The Margin of Safety

One of Buffett's core principles is the concept of the "margin of safety." This is the difference between the intrinsic value of a company and its market price. Buffett's rule of thumb is to only invest in a company when the market price is significantly below its intrinsic value. By doing so, he builds a protective buffer against market volatility and unforeseen downturns.

Diversification and Concentration

Buffett's approach to diversification differs from conventional wisdom. He advocates for concentrated investments in companies that you truly understand and believe in. By concentrating your investments in a select few companies, you can better manage and monitor their performance, reducing the risk of spreading yourself too thin.

Staying Informed and Disciplined

Buffett's risk management strategy also involves staying well-informed about the companies he invests in. He and his team regularly analyze financial statements, industry trends, and competitive dynamics. Additionally, they maintain discipline when it comes to buying and selling decisions. Emulating this disciplined approach can help you avoid impulsive decisions driven by market emotions.

Hedging and Insurance

While Buffett primarily relies on the quality of his investments as a hedge against risk, he also uses financial instruments like derivatives to manage risk on a larger scale within Berkshire Hathaway. He likens these instruments to insurance policies for his investments. We explore how these tools can be applied by individual investors on a more limited scale.

Psychological Resilience

Lastly, we delve into the psychological aspect of risk management. Buffett's unwavering confidence in his investments, even during market downturns, showcases his psychological resilience. We discuss techniques for maintaining a calm and rational mindset in the face of market fluctuations.

Practical Exercises and Tips

To conclude the chapter, we provide practical exercises and tips for implementing Buffett's risk management strategies in your own investment portfolio. These include assessing your investments for a margin of safety, creating a watchlist of companies you understand, and developing a disciplined investment routine.

Chapter 10: Learning from Mistakes: Warren's Investment Blunders and Lessons

Warren Buffett, often hailed as one of the greatest investors of all time, has certainly enjoyed his fair share of investment success. However, like any journey to greatness, his path has been paved with its fair share of missteps and mistakes. In this chapter, we'll delve into some of Warren's investment blunders and the valuable lessons we can glean from them.

The Oracle's Imperfections

Before we explore Warren Buffett's errors, it's essential to acknowledge that even the best investors are not infallible. Buffett himself has openly admitted to making mistakes throughout his career. He often quips that he's learned the most from his errors, and his willingness to share these lessons is part of what makes him such an invaluable teacher.

Case Study: Dexter Shoe Company

One of Buffett's most notable blunders was his investment in Dexter Shoe Company. In 1993, Berkshire Hathaway acquired the Maine-based shoe manufacturer for stock valued at $433 million. Unfortunately, Dexter Shoe eventually proved to be a failing business, and its value was written down to zero. Buffett openly acknowledges this mistake, calling it a "$400 million loss of your money."

Lessons Learned

Warren Buffett's Dexter Shoe investment provides several crucial lessons.

1 .Humility and Accountability

Even the most successful investors can make costly mistakes. Buffett's willingness to admit his errors and take responsibility for them demonstrates the importance of humility and accountability in investing.

2. Avoiding Overconfidence

Buffett's decision to invest in Dexter Shoe may have been influenced by overconfidence. It's essential to maintain a healthy dose of skepticism and thoroughly assess investment opportunities, regardless of your track record.

3. The Importance of Due Diligence

Dexter Shoe's decline highlighted the significance of thorough due diligence. Investors should conduct rigorous research and analysis before committing capital to any investment, no matter how promising it may seem.

4. The Value of Long-Term Perspective

While Dexter Shoe was a significant loss, Buffett's long-term perspective allowed him to recover from this mistake. He emphasizes that learning from failures is essential for long-term success.

Applying the Lessons

As readers aspiring to emulate Warren Buffett's success, it's crucial to internalize these lessons:

- Embrace humility and recognize that even the best investors make mistakes.

- Guard against overconfidence and maintain a critical eye in your investment decisions.

- Prioritize due diligence, conducting thorough research and analysis before investing.

- Remember that investing is a long-term endeavor, and setbacks are part of the journey to financial success.

By learning from Warren Buffett's mistakes and applying these lessons, you can navigate the world of investing with greater wisdom and resilience.

Chapter 11: Warren's Reading List: Developing a Lifelong Learning Habit

Warren Buffett is often referred to as one of the most voracious readers in the world of finance. His reading habits are legendary, and they have played a significant role in shaping his investment philosophy and overall success. In this chapter, we'll delve into the importance of reading and how you can develop a lifelong learning habit, just like Warren Buffett.

The Power of Books

Books have been a constant companion throughout Warren Buffett's life. He once famously said, "Read 500 pages like this every day. That's how knowledge works. It builds up, like compound interest." Here's why books are such a powerful tool for learning:

1. Access to Knowledge

Books provide access to a wealth of knowledge on a wide range of topics. Whether you're interested in finance, history, science, or philosophy, there's a book that can deepen your understanding.

2. Learning from Experts

Books are a way to learn from the experts. You can gain insights from the greatest minds in various fields without ever meeting them in person.

3. Developing Critical Thinking

Reading encourages critical thinking. It allows you to analyze different perspectives and form your own opinions, a skill crucial for successful investing.

Warren's Reading Habits

Warren Buffett's reading habits are nothing short of extraordinary. Here's a glimpse into how he approaches reading:

1. A Daily Ritual

Buffett dedicates a significant portion of his day to reading. He sets aside time every day to immerse himself in books, newspapers, and reports.

2. Wide Range of Topics

Buffett's reading is not limited to finance and investing. He reads newspapers from cover to cover, devours annual reports of companies, and delves into various subjects, from biographies to economics.

3. Taking Notes

Buffett takes notes while reading. He jots down ideas, insights, and questions that come to mind. This practice helps him retain and apply what he learns.

4. Continuous Learning

Warren Buffett's learning doesn't stop. He has stated that he spends about 80% of his working day reading and thinking. This dedication to continuous learning has been a cornerstone of his success.

Developing Your Lifelong Learning Habit

Now that you understand the importance of reading and how Warren Buffett approaches it, let's explore how you can develop your own lifelong learning habit:

1. Set Aside Time

Allocate dedicated time each day for reading. Start with as little as 15 minutes and gradually increase it. Consistency is key.

2. Diversify Your Reading List

Don't limit yourself to one genre or subject. Read broadly. Explore topics that interest you and those that challenge your thinking.

3. Take Notes

Keep a notebook or digital note-taking tool handy while you read. Jot down key takeaways, questions, and ideas that come to mind.

4. Join a Book Club

Consider joining a book club or discussion group. Engaging with others about what you've read can deepen your understanding and provide fresh perspectives.

5. Read with Purpose

Have a goal when you read. Whether it's to gain knowledge in a specific area or to explore a new subject, reading with purpose enhances the value of your reading time.

Warren Buffett's lifelong commitment to learning through reading is a testament to the transformative power of books. By emulating his habits and incorporating them into your daily routine, you can embark on a journey of continuous self-improvement and intellectual growth. Remember, as Buffett himself once said, "The more you learn, the more you'll earn."

Chapter 12: Financial Literacy Essentials: Buffet-Style Money Management

Warren Buffett's financial success isn't just about picking the right stocks; it's also deeply rooted in his keen financial literacy and savvy money management. In this chapter, we'll delve into the essential financial principles that have shaped Buffett's wealth-building journey and explore how you can apply them to your own financial life.

The Foundation of Financial Literacy

Warren Buffett once said, "The best investment you can make is in yourself." This wisdom underscores the importance of financial education as the bedrock of smart money management. To follow in Buffett's footsteps, you must first build a strong foundation in financial literacy.

1. Understand the Basics

Start by familiarizing yourself with fundamental financial concepts such as budgeting, saving, and debt management. Take the time to learn how to read financial statements, understand investment terminology, and grasp the fundamentals of economics.

2. Embrace Lifelong Learning

Buffett is known for his voracious reading habit, especially when it comes to financial and economic literature. Make reading and continuous learning a part of your daily routine. Explore books, articles, and online resources to stay informed about the ever-changing financial landscape.

Principles of Buffet-Style Money Management

Warren Buffett's approach to managing his personal finances is characterized by simplicity and discipline. Let's examine some of the key principles that define his money management strategy:

1. Live Below Your Means

Buffett's frugal lifestyle is a testament to his commitment to living below his means. He has consistently advised against extravagant spending and excessive debt. By adopting a similar mindset, you can free up more capital for investments and financial security.

2. Prioritize Long-Term Wealth

Buffett's focus on long-term wealth creation is a cornerstone of his financial philosophy. Instead of seeking short-term gains, he emphasizes the importance of patience and compounding over time. This approach aligns with the principles of value investing, which prioritize the intrinsic value of assets.

3. Diversify Thoughtfully

While Buffett believes in concentration when it comes to his stock investments, he also emphasizes the importance of diversification in other areas of his portfolio. This includes holding cash and bonds to provide stability during market downturns.

4. Avoid High-Fee Investments

Buffett is known for his disdain for high-fee investment products like actively managed mutual funds. He advocates for low-cost, passive index funds as a way to achieve broad market exposure while minimizing fees.

5. Focus on Tax Efficiency

Buffett's tax-efficient investing strategies have helped him maximize his returns. Understanding the tax implications of your investments and making strategic decisions can significantly impact your after-tax returns.

Building Your Financial Future

Warren Buffett's financial literacy and money management principles provide a roadmap for building and preserving wealth over a lifetime. As you embrace these principles and commit to ongoing financial education, you'll be better equipped to make informed financial decisions and secure your financial future.

This journey isn't solely about amassing wealth; it's also about using your financial resources wisely, giving back to society, and leaving a lasting legacy. In the following chapters, we'll explore these aspects of Buffett's life and philosophy, helping you further align your journey with his remarkable legacy.

Chapter 13: The Art of Shareholder Activism: Owning a Piece of the Pie

Warren Buffett's success as an investor extends beyond merely buying stocks; it includes actively participating in the companies he invests in. This chapter delves into the concept of shareholder activism and how you, as an investor, can leverage your ownership stake to influence positive change within companies.

Understanding Shareholder Activism

Shareholder activism involves using your rights and influence as a shareholder to advocate for changes within a company. While Warren Buffett is not traditionally seen as an activist investor in the aggressive sense, his approach to engaging with companies has had a significant impact. Here's how you can embrace shareholder activism in your investment journey:

1. Know Your Rights

Start by understanding your rights as a shareholder. These rights typically include voting at shareholder meetings, receiving company reports, and voicing concerns.

2. Choose Your Battles Wisely

Not every issue warrants activist engagement. Buffett himself has advised against becoming involved in every shareholder dispute. Focus on issues that are material to the company's long-term performance and align with your investment thesis.

3. Engage Constructively

Shareholder activism doesn't mean confrontation. Buffett's approach is often characterized by private discussions with management rather than public clashes. Engage with the company's leadership in a constructive and respectful manner.

4. Collaborate with Like-Minded Investors

Pooling resources and collaborating with other shareholders who share your concerns can amplify your impact. Buffett has occasionally partnered with other investors to push for changes.

5. Advocate for Sustainable Growth

Warren Buffett's approach to activism often centers on preserving and enhancing long-term value. Encourage the company to focus on sustainable growth strategies that benefit all shareholders over time.

Case Studies in Shareholder Activism

To illustrate the power of shareholder activism, this chapter will delve into case studies where Warren Buffett played a role in influencing company decisions. These case studies may include instances of governance reforms, capital allocation changes, or management transitions driven by Buffett's involvement.

Implementing Shareholder Activism in Your Portfolio

Concluding this chapter, we'll explore practical steps you can take to integrate shareholder activism into your investment strategy. This includes:

- Researching and identifying companies where your ownership can make a difference.

- Learning the art of effective communication with company leadership.

- Recognizing when to escalate your efforts or, when necessary, divest from a company that doesn't align with your principles.

Warren Buffett's approach to shareholder activism showcases that owning a piece of a company is more than just holding shares; it's about actively participating in its success. By understanding the principles of shareholder activism and applying them thoughtfully, you can make a positive impact on the companies you invest in, while also safeguarding your financial interests.

Chapter 14: Giving Back with a Purpose: Philanthropy and Social Responsibility

Warren Buffett, often called the "Oracle of Omaha," is renowned not just for his investing acumen but also for his deep commitment to philanthropy and social responsibility. In this chapter, we explore the significance of giving back with purpose and how you can incorporate philanthropic principles into your life.

The Power of Purposeful Philanthropy

Warren Buffett's approach to philanthropy is characterized by thoughtful giving and a dedication to making a lasting impact. He once famously said, "I want to give my kids just enough so that they would feel that they could do anything, but not so much that they would feel like doing nothing." This sentiment underscores the importance of instilling purpose in your philanthropic efforts.

* Defining your philanthropic mission: Take the time to identify the causes and issues that resonate with you personally. What are the social or environmental

problems you feel most passionate about addressing?

* Setting clear goals: Just as you set financial goals for your investments, establish specific, measurable objectives for your philanthropic endeavors. What impact do you hope to achieve, and how will you measure it?

Buffett's Philanthropic Pledge

Warren Buffett made headlines when he pledged to donate the majority of his wealth to charitable causes through the Bill and Melinda Gates Foundation and other organizations. This act of generosity reflects his commitment to using wealth for the greater good.

* The Giving Pledge: Learn about the Giving Pledge, an initiative co-founded by Warren Buffett and Bill and Melinda Gates, which encourages billionaires to commit to giving away the majority of their wealth.

* Effective altruism: Explore the concept of effective altruism, which involves making deliberate, well-informed choices to maximize the positive impact of your philanthropic efforts.

Strategies for Impactful Giving

Giving back isn't just about writing checks; it's about creating meaningful change. Buffett's philanthropic strategies can inspire your own approach.

* Leveraging your expertise: Consider how your unique skills and knowledge can be applied to effect positive change. For example, if you have a background in finance, you could volunteer to help nonprofits with financial management.

* Collaborative philanthropy: Buffett's partnerships with other philanthropists, like the Gates Foundation, demonstrate the power of collaboration. Explore opportunities to work with others who share your philanthropic goals.

Social Responsibility Beyond Philanthropy

Buffett's commitment to social responsibility extends beyond charitable giving. He emphasizes the importance of ethical business practices and corporate governance.

* Responsible investing: Learn about socially responsible investing (SRI) and how you can align your investments with your values by supporting companies that prioritize sustainability and ethical conduct.

* Advocacy and activism: Consider engaging in advocacy efforts to address social and environmental issues. Your voice and actions can contribute to positive change on a larger scale.

Making Your Mark

Remember that your actions, no matter how big or small, can leave a lasting impact. Warren Buffett's legacy isn't just about his wealth; it's about his dedication to making the world a better place. By following in his footsteps and giving back with a purpose, you can create a legacy that reflects your values and inspires others to do the same.

Chapter 15: Creating Your Legacy: Leaving a Lasting Impact Like Warren Buffett

Warren Buffett's legacy extends far beyond his immense wealth and investment prowess. It's a testament to his values, principles, and the positive impact he's had on countless individuals and society as a whole. In this final chapter, we explore how you can embark on your own journey to create a lasting legacy inspired by Buffett.

1. The Concept of Legacy

Legacy isn't just about accumulating wealth; it's about the mark you leave on the world. It's the values, principles, and contributions that outlive you. Legacy encompasses not only financial success but also your impact on your community, family, and the causes you hold dear.

2. Defining Your Legacy

Begin by asking yourself some essential questions:

- What do you stand for?

- What causes or issues are close to your heart?

- How do you want to be remembered by your loved ones and the world at large?

Your legacy is deeply personal and should align with your values and passions.

3. Philanthropy and Giving Back

Warren Buffett's dedication to philanthropy is a cornerstone of his legacy. Consider how you can make a positive difference through charitable giving. Whether it's through financial donations, volunteering, or using your skills to benefit others, philanthropy allows you to leave a meaningful mark on the world.

4. Mentoring and Passing on Knowledge

One way to leave a lasting legacy is by sharing your knowledge and expertise with others. Mentoring and teaching can have a profound impact on individuals and society as a whole. Consider how you can be a mentor or educator in your field of expertise.

5. Ethical and Sustainable Business Practices

Buffett's commitment to ethical business practices sets an example for all aspiring leaders. By conducting your professional life with integrity and sustainability in mind, you contribute to a legacy of responsible entrepreneurship.

6. Family and Relationships

Your legacy also extends to your family and personal relationships. Invest time in nurturing meaningful connections with loved ones and instilling values that will be carried forward by future generations.

7. Measuring Impact

Legacy isn't measured solely by the scale of your actions but by the depth of their impact. Keep in mind that even small acts of kindness and positive influence can have a ripple effect.

8. Staying Committed

Creating a lasting legacy is a lifelong endeavor. Stay committed to your values and principles, adjusting your actions as needed to align with your evolving vision.

9. Your Legacy, Your Story

Consider documenting your journey and the values that drive you. Your story can inspire others to embark on their own paths toward creating meaningful legacies.

10. Embracing Change

Finally, remember that legacies can evolve over time. Embrace change, adapt to new challenges, and remain open to opportunities to make a difference.

As you reflect on Warren Buffett's remarkable legacy and embark on your own journey to leave a lasting impact, keep in mind that your legacy is a reflection of your unique qualities, values, and contributions to the world. By following in Buffett's footsteps and applying the principles discussed in this book, you have the potential to create a legacy that will inspire and benefit generations to come.